To Frank
And you can do
it too !

Best wishes,

Faye x

Peripheral

FAYE BOLAND

GW00771114

First Published in 2018 by The Manuscript Publisher

ISBN: 978-1-911442-15-8

A CIP Catalogue record for this book is available from
the National Library

Typesetting, page design and layout by
DocumentsandManuscripts.com

Cover design by Jo-Anne Yelen
Photography by SallyAnn Boland

Published, printed and bound in Ireland

Peripheral

A *SiarScéal* Publication

sponsored by

The Manuscript Publisher

www.SiarSceal.com

Acknowledgements

My thanks to the editors of the following publications, where some of these poems were first published: *The Shop* (Editors, John and Hilary Wakeman), *Orbis* (Editor, Carole Baldock), *The Galway Review* (Editor, Máire Holmes), *Tales From the Forest* (Editor, Rose Fortune), *Three Drops From A Cauldron* (Editor, Kate Garrett), *The Curlew* (Editor, Lynn Parr), *Headstuff* (Editor, Alvy Carragher), *All the Sins* (Editors, Lisa Davison and Sinead Keegan), *Skylight 47* (Editors, Kevin O'Shea, Susan Lindsay and Nicki Griffin), *The Weary Blues* (Editor, Emily Cullen) and *Literature Today* (Editor, Dr. Pradeep Chaswal).

Peripheral won the Hanna Greally International Literary Award 2017.

Silver Bracelet was shortlisted for the Poetry on the Lake XIII International Competition in 2013.

I am very grateful to SiarScéal Festival for making available the funding for this project, which is sponsored by The Manuscript Publisher.

Particular thanks are owed to Eileen F. Connolly, Annemarie Ní Churreain and Jack McAuliffe who read this manuscript from beginning to end and offered numerous suggestions to improve it. Thanks also to the members of Clann na Farraige writers group and my family for their helpful comments on various poems over the years. I would also like to thank John

W. Sexton, Máire Holmes, Eileen Sheehan, Noel King and Noel O'Regan for their support and advice on my work.

Contents

Bile*

The acorn is my talisman
I squeeze it in the palm
of my hand; remember
you rubbing a buddha's belly,
as he sat cross-legged on your dressing-table,
the scent of incense rising
like charmed snakes.
Your polished nails dealt my cards:
the King of Wands.

You prophesied print and travel,
children, a King. The grey city
where you wore your perfume
like a philtre was cold as concrete.
I saw no King, heard no birdsong.

Then you took me to a field.
A golden oak, king of trees,
leaves the colour of sunshine,
stretched out its arms,
ready to embrace the world.

And at our feet a four-leafed clover.

* A Sacred Tree. *Old Moore's Almanac* describes bile
as individual trees that stood out in the landscape, as
being remarkable perhaps, for their size or shape, or
the place in which they grew.

1992

was when I ate my first chip butty, acquired a taste
for curry houses that dished up biryanis, lassi,
lived in a terraced house near little Beirut,
my landlord, Mr Woodhead, his caretaker, Mrs
    Hoodless.
I walked through the park where students were raped
every weekend. My Grandmother, watching the
reports on Sky News, begged my father to bring me
    home.
1992 was the year I knew methadone users
with smack-head friends, who trickled in and out,
lifting my ersatz silver when I left my flat unlocked.
There were no patisseries in this city, just run-down
    cafés
where pensioners drank tea from polystyrene cups,
ate toasted teacakes. I burrowed into postgraduate
    textbooks,
devoured the advertisements, like mini-movies, on
    TV.
Walked anonymously in the University campus,
Frank O'Connor, my companion, sitting on my
    bedside locker
when I returned at night. My attic window looked
    down on the city,
coal-black, cold as steel. In 1992, as the Fokker 50
rattled over England, I looked down on one
    continuous housing estate
stretching east from Manchester; row after row,
like combed hair, perfectly parted.

Lost in the Crowd

On weekday mornings
she joins the cortège
of cadaver-filled cars:
a procession made up of bodies
still not awake but silently
dreading another work day.
Car light-eyes illuminate the dark
as they slowly stop-start,
winding their way to the
mass grave office where
nobody feels alive.

On Saturdays, she takes
the train to town, passes
the hours window-shopping,
being jostled by crowds.
Sipping coffee, she watches
the multicoloured plaid
of aimless browsers weaving
through focused shopaholics.

On Sundays, seated on a hard
pew, her eyes digest couples
shepherding children into Saint Brigid's
then home for Sunday dinner.
From her flat, she sees
driveways belch out cars,
congest the streets, as families gather

for roast beef and Yorkshire pudding,
more appetising than her microwaved
meal for one.

Snapshot

From space today, Dublin looks green
with mouldy spores of white lights,
where commuters have risen early
to catch the Luas or Dart,
as bound soon for city centre
shoppers boil their kettles,
press lists into notepads.

The International Space Station
is a warm 23 degrees, while
below in Dublin, a homeless man,
frozen this December morning,
wakes to a street-cleaner's cart
rattling near the doorway where he sleeps.
He squeezes circulation
into his toes and fingers, checks
his friend is still alive.

As Astronaut Randy Bresnik tweets
his panoramic Dublin snapshot,
Christmas shoppers shuttle past
the nameless homeless man,
inconsequential as a wrapper discarded
on the street. Pull focus on one
of the one hundred and eighty-four
sleeping rough in Dublin, not visible
in Bresnik's satellite photo.

Tonight, when shoppers and commuters
ease into fire-warmed armchairs

and Bresnik hooks his sleeping bag to the wall
after Skyping his loved ones on Earth,
more than three thousand faceless, nameless children
and five thousand faceless, nameless adults
will be officially homeless*. Outside,
the city's locked doors.

   * Figures for February 2018 reveal that 9,870 people
are now homeless.

Pulse

Warm as a timber fire,
your basenotes

travel along
invisible modes, fibres

at the speed of light.
I am mellowed

by the tempo
of your speech

light, *vif.*
My words tinkle,

a *decrescendo*.
Sentences step out

of the silence,
waltz down the cables,

tap out
fibre optic pulses,

the blood-red
of my heart,

orange sparks.

Sunday Lie-in

Awareness bubbles
as consciousness slowly surfaces.
I roll into you, your heat,
eyes stuck closed.
Your hand glides
over my hair;
fingertips trace the ridge
of my cheekbone;
the dip before my lips
puff up. I blissfully shut out
the clock's soft tick,
the honey'd haze
of early morning sunlight,
drift away into ethereal sleep.

My Shadow

an unwelcome guest
sits with me at meals,
encouraging me to
eat for two.

amorphous,
talks me out of
vigorous exercise,
preferring an oversized
frame to slink
in and out of.
When I walk
it dogs my heels,
slows me down.

nags me with
doubts as I contrive
to succeed and, descending
stealthily like a smog,
obscures my purpose.

derides my flat notes
and, without an original
thought of its own,
resents my progress.

skulks away, cuckolded
when you lie with me

and, thanks to your love-tinted eyes,
(or perhaps the lack of sunlight)
I manage to shrink a size.

Mermaid on a Rock

Hangs, slightly tilted,
behind the two-seater sofa.
A mermaid with cascading
frond-blonde hair,
arms outstretched.
Tail, peduncle, flukes dangle
above a seaweed-green ocean.

After the adult exhibition
where it was tagged,
Not for Sale,
you hung it and I smiled,
intending to move it
to the playroom
when I got a chance.

I shed the throws,
changed the sofas.
You moved from art
to music to sport and
on to computer games, mobile phones.
I keep meaning to move
the mermaid, so incongruous
with the soothing, oil-painted flowers
but your objections are trenchant

and all too soon, you'll have gone.

Painting of Ardtully House

Turrets stand sentry
over ladies riding side-saddle.
The great oak door
conceals the house's treasures:
gilt-framed portraits of
snub-nosed ancestor-dandies
hung on wood-panelled walls,
corniced ceilings looking
down on oriental rugs,
clothing naked flagstone floors.
Flamboyant velvet curtains trail
from pelmet-mantled windows.

Roused from four-poster beds,
there was no time to save
the silver spoons, bone china
as flames licked the polished mahogany,
charred chaises longues
on which ladies languished,
expectant in their ascendancy.

Burned back to bare brick,
another piece of our heritage was lost
for freedom.

Ardtully House, built in 1847, replaced a number of
earlier structures dating as far back as 1214. The
House was burnt in 1921.

Heritage

When garnet blackberries dangled like earrings
on bramble-blanketed hedgerows,
little purple fingertips picked them
in bucket loads. Slashed down
to expose stone walls, bleached white
as perfect as veneered Hollywood teeth.
Concrete contenders made for tidy towns and tourists.

Airplanes droned, cement mixers churned.
Lilies were gilded, fields carpeted in concrete.
Developers jumped aboard the gravy train,
pimpling the countryside with a rash of houses,
the landscape becoming indelibly scarred;
towns and villages now pockmarked with housing
    estates
that ooze two decades of profligacy and waste.

Dust to dust, the developers have gone
the dinosaur diggers extinct.
Rats banquet on uncollected garbage, cesspits
of neglect where service charges remain unpaid.
Half-incubated houses haunt weed-infested
ghost estates, eerily echoing earlier prophesies
that they rested on fragile foundations.
Mortgagees constricted by the threat of foreclosure,
a hangman's noose woven from credit, tax breaks
and greed.

The bramble's tentacles slither slowly over bricks and
    mortar.

House of Horrors

In Betty's bloodbath eyeballs bob
with chopped off hands and feet.
She stirs her ragoût, dangles
her husband's matted hair, tells how
she scalped him when he came home
late for dinner.

Next, the blood-spattered butcher
wields his meat cleaver over severed
limbs. Zombie schoolgirls grab
at passers-by. In a side room,
a gunshot shatters a skull, splatters
blood and bone.

In another, a caged beast grunts,
is carted off by white-coated wardens,
beaten. A sulphurous smoke fingers its way
down the dark claustrophobic corridor
where hooded ghouls jump out, terrorize.
Next an exorcism.

Welcome to the House of Horrors.
Admission 5 euros.
Not for the faint-hearted.

Pirate

You picture yourself riding the waves
in a timber galleon. Torches blazing,
skull and crossbones waving,
sporting an eyepatch, feathered hat,
cutlass in hand. Giving orders like
chips and sausages for supper, an
unending supply of chocolate caramels
and popcorn. If only you'd been born a pirate
like your Dad, from abroad, rough and ready,
giving orders, brawling. But you're just a boy
born to a mother bred on manners
and you have to stay seated at the table,
eat all your meat and veg, use a knife and fork,
sit still, not grab, say please and thank you.

In your dreams, you sail around the world,
kill with cannon, maim with swords.
At night, I hear you whimper, crying out with fear.
Running to your side, I scoop you up,
move you to my big warm bed, stroke
your silk-soft hair, marshmallow face until
you close your sleepy eyes,
ready to resume your battle
so rudely interrupted.

Compensation*

You stripped me
of my childhood,
my future.

When I vomited
up the taste
of sex and sweat

you looked away,
patted down your hair
and walked out.

Now I'll take your creditworthiness,
your good name,
leave you bankrupt, *child abuser*.

An eye for an eye?
There will be no justice
in this life,

Atonement will be
your screams
from Hell.

* On 6 December 2016, *The Irish Times* reported that
a child abuse victim had brought proceedings against
her attacker in order to have him declared bankrupt
and force the sale of his assets. The assailant had
failed to pay compensation of €21,000, awarded by

the High Court in Northern Ireland and legal costs of
€43,000 incurred by his victim.

Silver Bracelet

The jeweller and I guessed your size:
a bespoke bracelet, name and date
of birth engraved, polished silver
a mirror for your perfect face.

On a pillow of cotton wool it lay,
expectant in its box, like you.
The engraving immortalised your date of
death. You wore it to the grave.

Amphibian

Amphibious from the moment
you swam from amniotic fluid
into the cradle of my arms,
gulped your first breath.

Derided for your waddle, flat
webbed feet, you learned to blow bubbles
in the bathroom sink, head ducked
underwater like a cygnet searching.

Now you ride the waves
in a wooden boat,
fronds of red hair
flapping in sea-spray. Perched

in position, you grip the oar,
heave its weight and as it cuts
through salt water, I see you gliding
into your destiny.

Violets

After Maude Jane Delap, 1866-1953

Valentia. Waves
flung against the rocks.
Plumes of sea-spray,
a biting wind.

He comes by steam train,
his team of scientists
ferried to the island
in wooden rowboats.

She sends him violets
every year on his birthday.

Her brothers away at school,
she learns at home,
combs the beaches,
collects samples.

Anemones, jellyfish
sashay in bell jars.
The house smells of low tide
and arum lilies.

She sends him violets
every year on his birthday.

She writes by candlelight.
Papers rustle.

Her work grows in stature.
Oxygen bubbles in bell jars.

She, forbidden to leave home
without a husband.
He leaves behind a void
no islander can fill.

She sends him violets
every year on his birthday.

Choctaw Girl

I stumbled upon you,
a piece of driftwood
wedged on a rocky shore.
Your voice wept
like advancing waves.
Your footsteps were
the sorrowful drum
of rain on sand.

Your ancestors heard
my forefathers fall
silently as feathers.
Their largesse
quivered our waters, echoes
in the conch's sea-swish.

You recognised my ancestry,
saw I'd become a quisling,
forfeiting my homeland.
Blood-brothers from the start
we wove a plait of friendship
from mutual displacement,
two lost spirits searching
for a settled heart.

Prayer

Crowded like beans
in ful medames*, we bob
towards freedom,
wind-burned, sun-beaten.

Our thirst is sea-blue,
hunger unquenched.
Salt stings parched lips
that pray for Allah's mercy:

*Allah, grant us the good of this world and that of
the Hereafter and save us from the torture of
Hell.*

Listless, we drift
through a no-man's land
of sea and sky,
silent between prayers

until another woman
screams, and our prayers
rise, loud enough
to reach Allah's gates:

*Allah, grant us the good of this world and that of
the Hereafter and save us from the torture of
Hell.*

*Ful medames is a fava bean stew eaten in Syria.

Home

is a field, stretched over red sandstone,
overgrown with ferns, prickled with gorse,
where my father dreamed a bungalow would sit,
on which stands a peak-white mansion.
I painted its fence tudor black,
varnished floorboards I mop and wax.

is a doorstep where an aged dog dozes,
rising on stiff legs at the sound of my car.
A view of a clothes line where tiny trousers kick
and frilly dresses swing. Where trumpet-like flowers,
resplendent with colour, peer in from window ledges.

is the waltz of garlic and onions,
a six-seater table, scuffed, with white rings.
The wail of a violin not quite in tune,
the hum of a fridge while everyone sleeps.

Peripheral

My roof is the sky,
the wind my walls.

Every night it blows
the same word:

Homeless.
Homeless.

In winter it skins me.
I hide in my hood,

tuck my knees
into myself

but still I burn.
I am empty, on the edge

of danger, a genie
on a cardboard carpet.

Hopeless, I dive
into the bottom

of a bottle, take comfort
in its warm glow.

See the stars shiver.

Würzburg 1942

In the end,
they took our keys,
a list of property,
drove us out
of our last refuge,
the cemetery.
Two thousand of us,
our few remains in bags,
boarded the trains
eastbound.

Before the dark sky
glowed with yellow stars,
they banqueted together,
toasted their Fuehrer,
slopped beer.
Raucous laughter, bawdy jokes
echoed in the Residenz.
Tiepolo's fresco looked down
the marble staircase:
Himmel auf Erden

Heaven on Earth.

Big Chef, Little Chef

Half-awake, half-asleep
the two trundle
down the stairs
in matching blue pjs,
enter the linoed set
of *Big Chef, Little Chef*.
The camera begins to roll.

Good morning boys and girls,
says Little Chef. *Today we will make
porridge*. Big Chef adds,
*first, we pour porridge flakes
into a clean bowl and add milk.*
Little Chef stirs in the milk with a spoon
and in his best BBC voice says,
*Now, Big Chef will place the porridge
in the microwave for 2 minutes.*

After the *bing*, Little Chef stirs in
an overflowing spoon of honey,
ignoring the droplets
that scatter over the table
between stray porridge flakes.
That's all for today boys and girls, he says.
Tune in next week to Big Chef and Little Chef.

Little Chef is too busy eating
to offer further commentary.
From the wall, the Sacred Heart glows
through the morning's dim light,

eyes smile on a sleepy stepfather
pouring boiling water
onto his coffee granules.

First Flight

The smell of coffee,
tar-thick, pungent,
chokes you, like your siblings
names, too many to list
without thinking,
deep pain.

Served by a beauty pageant
hostess, she sashays
through the cabin aisle
tries to comfort you, alone,
legs too short
to reach the cabin floor.

The propellers drone fretfully,
churn through cloud faces.
You see Mama in curlers,
slippers, contemplating
the words she'll write.
The engine rattles your mind.

Coffee still holds the taste
of that terrible flight.

Oblation

In music class you'd act the fool,
make us laugh.
The Earth was yours to inherit
before your mind
started to play tricks on you.

Drove you off the road, wrecking
a row of cars. Believing you were Jesus
you'd strip naked,
wander desolate hills,
gorse thorns ripping your skin.

Destitute on the Kilburn High Road,
your faculties scattered like seeds,
on the stony ground where you sat.
On the last day, you waded out of your depth,
offered yourself up.

The Ubiquitous Dawn Dairies Milkman

I see him at garages,
supermarkets, corner shops,
as I squeeze out of
bottle-necked school traffic,
filter into fast-flowing
town centre shoppers.
A white-coated apparition
with a halo of white hair,
he glows brighter and whiter
than the early morning shufflers,
the mid-day rushers.
In a flash, I see him
unloading crates from his dirty truck,
creating a cold ripple
as he walks.

Travelling alone,
the sight of him is as comforting
as a mug of strong tea.
I wave to this nameless milkman
and his return salute slices
through the chilly air,
his smile iridescent.

In dependence

When you see me waiting at the school gate,
a switch flicks and your eyes light up
like light bulbs; a slice of melon smile
divides your face, reaches each ear.

I wave. You push your way through the
stream of kids, call my name.
Excitement tumbles from your lips.
As you reach me you stop short of
the anticipated embrace, grab a friend.

The schoolbag's thrown into my arms.
I try to keep apace as you race each other
to the playground. I am all yours,
grateful for the acknowledgment
and happy to follow.

January Rust

Rain speckling my glasses, I walk to town
this Friday evening. My spirit craves
the lubricating warmth of company but Christmas
    over,
tourists, students have drained away from narrow
    footpaths.
Traffic lights wait on green, an occasional car
swishes glistening streets. A spotlight
on the church front beams on a gauze of rain.
In the electrical shop, TV screens flash.

Pub windows show only bartenders
polishing glossy wood, brass. I spy
two men sitting rod-straight at a counter,
hours before regulars trickle in for last orders.
Trudging home, tongues of rain begin to sting.
I am revived by the smell of salt air.

Driving the Gap Road

November drizzle.
Four teenagers are steered home,
swaying at each bend. Complaints drone.
The odour of vinegar and ketchup.
Wheels swish on wet asphalt.
A burst of song, Madonna's *Into the Groove*.
The rain steps up a gear, drums on the roof.
Spirits soar above the clouds.

Twenty miles of road-ribbon;
we own each twist and turn.

Samhain 2016.
Wipers creak a winter heartbeat
as I navigate the twisted Gap Road.
At the roadside, shrivelled russet ferns
edge yellowed grasses,
roots immersed in bog.
Drenched sheep graze on ridges,
veined with overflowing streams.
A gnarled tree scratches.

Twenty miles of road-ribbon
I own each twist and turn.

Gorseland

After Ann Tuohy

Before fair day, she'd
scrub his pants and geansaí
on the washboard
with Sunlight soap,
pray he'd get a good price
for the sheep: enough to
buy shoes to keep the children's
feet from blistering.

She loved the honey'd smell
of laundered sheets left
to sun-dry on tufts of furze,
was grateful for her humble home
on mountainous land where only
sheep would grow.

Under her bed she kept a tea-chest,
a treasure trove of linen and lace,
relics of her time in America
before she was matched
to my grandfather – high-necked
blouses, swooshing skirts,
dancing shoes, dainty as a doll's.

Every now and then she'd
lay them out on the bed,
promise them to me
then fold each garment,

tuck it back in place,
perfume her tea-chest
with fresh mothballs.

Doppelganger

Doppelganger, my perfect match,
I long to roll into your springy softness,
feel your toes curling around mine.

I miss our comradeship
as we stepped out together,
our movements synchronized.

We weathered rainwater,
darting out of its path
like frogs jumping

to dry land. Warmed by
the aga's belly, we breathed
snakes of steam.

We hung out for hours,
side by side, swam like tadpoles
orbiting each other

till a black hole sucked you in.
Now I languish on the odd sock pile
while you exist forlorn in a parallel universe –

the twilight zone of inexplicably lost socks.

Little Maverick Hen

Little maverick hen,
undersized but valiant
scorns the hens,
overfed and unintelligent.
She nests with the ducks,
gobbles their food,
unfazed by their filthy water.

These shortening winter days,
she pecks purposefully,
an explorer searching out
her own terrain in the shrubs.
At night, as the hens
file into their coop,
she refuses to surrender
to the call to roost,
placing herself in the path
of unknown nocturnal terrors.

She waits for me each morning,
hopping impatiently,
every speckled feather
on her crested neck
unruffled.

Crow

Crow, tar-black coated, brill-slick
targets the carnage with bulbous eyes,
rodent entrails splattered on the road below.
Swoops down with caped wings,
stabs at his damned prey with charcoal beak,
curved like a sickle. Savagery disturbed
by oncoming cars, agitated wings ascend.
At the edge of the passing world he waits,
skims into the first gap, perfidious pilferer,
mocking with his caw-caw laugh.

Aftermath

Forked branches stab
the chilly air. I sit on cold
stone, watch children clamber
on rocks, unsettling the stillness
as their seagull-shrieks rise
in an airborne swirl.

Here *Darwin* bellowed,
uprooted titanic oaks,
flung interwoven debris,
plastic, seaweed
at the road's edge.
This freak-tide ribbon,
vestige of the flood's threat
before it scuttled away,
sucking the wind seaward.

Sky's the Limit

At 1,000 feet high, I have forgotten
my hour-long ascent along zig-zagging paths,
pebbled with sheep droppings, bees
roused from prickly heather beds
loop the looping, my teenage angst.

At 1,000 feet high, I can see
15 miles of baby blue bay push back
a cloudy horizon, slice through a landscape
of sheer purple mountains, rugged green islands
spat out along the way.

At 1,000 feet high, I see
my neighbourhood, the far-off town's church spire
climbing above the trees, all frozen like a modern-day
Constable or Turner scene, in which microscopic cars
creep like ants along the road.

At 1,000 feet high, I am mesmerised,
until the cold rock on which I sit
pulls me from my trance. My feet
are firmly rooted in the dusty ground.
My fingertips can almost touch the sky.

Thumbs Up

We haven't met in years.
You stop to greet me,
thumbs up, finger pointed towards the sky.
It's a nice day.

I smile, reply
with awkward gestures.
My response covers
like skin on milk.

My fingers move like ants:
I am going for a walk.
Then, grasshopper-quick,
I take off.

I see you again in the café,
watching shoppers scuttle by.
I stop to breathe in
a florist's display.

You wave, rub your heart, point
to the blossoms. I mirror your actions.
I would love to join you but again
I am choked.

So much to say
but I lack the tools

to convey what's buried
beneath the surface:

my gestures like midges hovering on top.

Swallows Return

Celebrating their arrival,
they flit, dive, skim
the terrain of red rock,
green and rhododendron,
pirouette upwards, start
again. Barometer of midges,
summer. No time to rest,
they feed on the wing,
cut up the sky with flashes
of metallic blue-black,
perform dizzying aerobatics.

Incredibly, they mapped their
route across the Tropics for food,
the ten thousand kilometre
journey home to last year's nest
of Muxnaw mud, tucked
into a corner of our shed.

Perfectly Blue

"Our relations with Germany are infinitely more friendly now than they have been for years… Never has the sky been more perfectly blue."

– David Lloyd George, January 1914

Never has the sky been
more perfectly blue,
unsullied by angry peaks
of exploding mines;
low-lying clouds
of mustard gas asphyxiating
the air.
There is yet
no endless buzz of bullets,
no craters gouged
by exploding shells,
no clap of grenades,
no hammer of machine guns,
no shrapnel which scatters
with the sound of shattering glass.
No screams,
as young men's limbs rip
from their bodies
as lives sink into mud.

Rock 'n' Roll Star

He's a rock 'n' roll star
though nobody knows it;
they walk on his dreams
but one day he'll show them.
When he stands on the stage
the crowd will adore him and
hysterical girls will scream
as they cry, bribing security
with a sly folded note.
After the show, he'll be papped
looking smug, with arms tentacled
'round supermodels who vye for a slice
of his fame and his life.

When no one is watching,
he nuzzles her neck,
slender and smooth, before he begins
gently plucking her strings.
Soon the chords are vibrating,
the volume is rising,
the music is smoking
and the temperature's soaring.
In the thrill of it all, he's visualising
being reclined on the sand
on some tropical island,
being handed an umbrella-topped
cocktail by a topless waitress
who's tall, tanned *and blonde*.

When he plays his guitar he's somebody
else. He forgets all his debts
and the stress of being idle.
He's living the dream, not trudging
through rain for welfare on a Wednesday,
that's all gone by Sunday.
Caught in the grip of the ashtray, his lonely
cigarette smoulders forgotten
as the music goes on and on
and on. Nothing else matters
when he plays his guitar but the thrill
of being a rock 'n' roll star.

Cupids

At the edge of town
        a constant beat.
                    Buses park,
        a queue waits.

Hair styled,
        tightest jeans,
                    doors open,
        lipstick checked.

Underage drinkers
        evade bouncers.
                    The stink
        of spilled beer.

Smoke-machine
        dance-floor,
                    purple rain-
        French kisses.

Derelict.
        A scooped-out shell.
                    Furniture flung,
        windows smashed.

Overgrown.
        Buddleia, ragwort,
                    briar, bursting
        into song.

John Joe

John Joe speeds down the
narrow lane, wearing his
grey caipín and dirty
polyester jacket, taking milk
to the creamery. Focused on
work, he slows for no one,
barely sees us, wheel-sized,
holding hands at the roadside.

He does not see my sister pull
me back towards the ditch,
drag me out, slime-coated, my
hair sprouting twigs and leaves.
Does not see my tomato face
when questioned by neighbours;
does not hear my refusal to admit
my downfall.

Domestic Goddess

Queen of Puddings,
she dumplings her casseroles,
croutons her soups,
makes loaves and fishes of
nature's seasonal offerings,
turns water into elderflower
wine. Her Formica shines as
chrome appliances mock
her surrender to shapelessness;
her form reflected like a cherry
on an enormous muffin.

Through steamy eyes
she remembers stick legs
pedalling, spokes whizzing,
freewheeling, as hair billowed
like sheets in the wind,
wolf whistles cheering her on.

Mystery

She's a mystery to him,
like the Bermuda Triangle,
the Immaculate Conception,
aliens.

The time she fritters
on the phone, at the hairdressers,
haemorrhaging money,
her monthly moods.

She's the wrecking ball of
a man's freedom, her duster, hoover
bulldozing the peaceful enjoyment
of his TV. An inferno
filling him with an insatiable thirst.

For the slightest transgression,
he'll pay. Freezing him with bitter
eyes, he'll face her gargoyle grimace,
and in her voice,
that sounds like breaking glass,
he'll hear his mother.

Sunday Best

For my mother

Mary Malone, B.T.A.*
has her own bathroom
with a clawfoot bath,
porcelain sink
to wash her hands in –
a notion she got
from her time in America.
Luxuries that we
readers of women's magazines
dream of; her neighbours who
freeze using the privy,
perform our ablutions in a washbowl,
bathe once a week in a tin bath
dragged in front of the open fire
that heats our water.
Though many envy
her good fortune, on a Sunday
you'd never know she was
a cut above the rest of us.
With my face shining from Pears soap,
sleek hair dressed in ribbons,
I show the world where I am headed
as I stride up the aisle, chin tilted skyward.

*Been To America

Hypochondriac

On those out-of-office Sundays,
he'd flag down a hapless tourist;
puff-panting, grab his hand,
asphyxiate him with the sour-milk
stench of overdue baths, dirty clothes.
He spoke the universally understood language
of imminent heart-failure
to those without a word of English.
Fleas hopping with delight
onto the newly upholstered interior,
they'd zoom from town to ours
for his umpteenth blood pressure check
of the week, having ignored repeated
diagnoses of good health.

Peering through the glossy-leaved bushes,
I'd see him stagger out the passenger side
as his chauffeur sped away; watch
this ragbag of rancid smells, exhortations,
weave the breadth of the tarmacadam drive,
my predicament washing over me like
cold water as our front door lock clicked.

Meadow Fresh

The floor smiles back
as you breeze in.
Orchid-scented floor cleaner
wafts up to meet you.
I greet you with a sigh.

My lips are rod straight;
back, bridge-bent.
Cut knuckles sting
in bleach-burned hands.
I lean on the mop.

In lacklustre eyes
you see today's struggle
to press a dirty house
into the shape of a meadow,
fragrant with flowers.

By nightfall, the rub
of your palms on my tired arches
wipes clean the pain,
all thoughts of unfinished work,
the walls that fence me in

until I am weightless,
brushed along by the swish
of meadow grass, through
cow parsley, ragged robin,
the scent of lus taghla,

and all is wildness
and fragrant and
I am smiling.

Weightless

i.m. Ebbo Lüttgen

Your ashes are warm,
as if you are still here.

They weigh heavy,
as if your bones

have not yet assumed
the shape of an urn.

As your ashes
are scattered

a biting wind
scoops them up.

You rise weightless,
unburdened by illness,

as if your spirit has wings
and you are flying

above the waves,
grey and foamy,

becoming part of
where you settle.

As if you are still here,
will always be here.

Good Intentions

The last time we met
I saw bony cheeks,
flesh eaten, pothole eyes.
Death had claimed your soul.
Calculating wastage,
your independence,
will to live against all odds,
I gave you six months more,
finalised arrangements
for our next dinner,
dashed out the door.

Our last minutes together
and I never held your cold hand,
touched the remaining tufts
of your hair.
I could have poured your drink,
taken you back to your
downy-duveted bed,
tucked you in.
Foolishly I agonised
over next week's dinner menu,
engagement broken.
Planned a small token,
never delivered.

Gretel's Return

For Kate McCann

No pebbles as markers,
not even a crumb
of hope as to your whereabouts,
dead or alive.

The soft, wrinkled sheet on which you lay
grew cold. Vanished
into the darkness, snatched
from your bed.

Hair torn out, flesh wasting
away from my skeletal frame,
terror nauseated
as the hours turned into days.

Time does not anaesthetise
my amputee's loss and pain,
heart's gaping hole,
as hair greys, days turn into years

and I am still waiting.

Mona Lisa

I have left the land of potatoes and butter. Here, people surge like a swollen river, grey, detritus-ridden. And everywhere, eyes. Mona Lisa, eye-spying cameras watch every step I take.

The eye of the clock I check against the train timetable. Lidded eyes that look away, at the floor, hiding in their newspapers. Four-eyed geeks on laptops. Children's eyes staring at deformities, differences. Kohl-rimmed eyes in burkas. Eyes that flirt from glossy magazines. The London Eye.

The eye of the storm that dumps its rain on the taxi roof, on the homeless man who sits on wet cardboard, faceless behind his hood. Bullseye: A coin thrown into his paper cup rattles the change inside. Cat's eyes amber the dark road. Headlights glare.

Pollution clouds the stars. You see them twinkle like eyes and think of me so far away. The receptionist at the check-in desk flutters her false eyelashes as she speaks. Elevator music pipes 'can't take my eyes off you'. I'll phone you later from my hotel room. First, I take some me-time, become an 'I' instead of insignificant 'other'. I transform from an amorphous mother into the shape of a woman. Lip-sticked and high-heeled. Eye-catching. I treat myself to a gin and tonic from the mini-bar. In the fridge back home the potatoes grow eyes, the milk sours.

Aberration

Maybe it's the fact that I'm done
with cities, hard-edged, stifling;
underground's rubber fumes,
the throng of people, din
and thrust of traffic,
nights pierced by sirens,
shouts and screams.

And city summers,
clothes stuck-to-skin,
concrete flashing heat.
Fear of strangers.
Adrenaline-pumping-over-the-shoulder
glancing, on-the-edge-of-nerves
alert for men who prey on lone women,
drunk women, women in cars.

I am at home in this place,
a theophany, pulsing slower
than a heartbeat. Concrete an aberration,
all is cloaked in green – forests, fields,
curved hills that roll down, touch the shore.
Here all is vibrant and alive,
hedgerows jewelled with fuchsia,
waves slurping rounded stones,
the hare who stares me in the eye
before lolloping off.

Homeward

I turn onto the Kilgarvan road,
reception lost, the outside world cut off.
The car is teased by corkscrew turns,
its roaring stops, the engine hums.
The sacred oak leans towards me,
waves me on, past endless fir-forests,
arrow-head bristles pointing proudly
skywards. Moss-blanketed walls
give way to brown-tufted drumlins,
a scrub-land of rushes, gorse. Candyfloss
clouds puff up, wash the windscreen
with a soft drizzle.
I am home.

Come Here, Robin

by **Katie Woolley** and **Paul Nicholls**

W
FRANKLIN WATTS
LONDON•SYDNEY

I held out a worm.

Come here, robin.

I held out a snail.

Come here, robin.

5

I held out a spider.

Come here, robin.

I held out a grasshopper.

Come here, robin.

I held out a slug.

Come here, robin.

11

I held out a caterpillar.

Come here, robin.

13

I held out a seed.

Come here, robin.

15

I held out a berry.

Come here, robin.

Story trail

Start

Start at the beginning of the
story trail. Ask your child to retell
the story in their own words,
pointing to each picture in turn
to recall the sequence of events.

Independent Reading

This series is designed to provide an opportunity for your child to read on their own. These notes are written for you to help your child choose a book and to read it independently.

In school, your child's teacher will often be using reading books which have been banded to support the process of learning to read. Use the book band colour your child is reading in school to help you make a good choice. *Come Here, Robin* is a good choice for children reading at Pink 1B in their classroom to read independently.

The aim of independent reading is to read this book with ease, so that your child enjoys the story and relates it to their own experiences.

About the book

In this story, a shy little robin lands in a garden looking for food. Can the little boy persuade the robin to take some?

Before reading

Help your child to learn how to make good choices by asking: "Why did you choose this book? Why do you think you will enjoy it?" Support your child to think about what they already know about the story context. Look at the cover together and ask: "What do you think the story will be about?" Read the title aloud and ask: "What time of year do you think the story is set in? Why might it be hard to find food at this time?"

Remind your child that they can try to sound out the letters to make a word if they get stuck.

Decide together whether your child will read the story independently or read it aloud to you. When books are short, as at Pink 1B, your child may wish to do both!

During reading

If reading aloud, support your child if they hesitate or ask for help by telling the word. Remind your child of what they know and what they can do independently.

If reading to themselves, remind your child that they can come and ask for your help if stuck.

After reading:

Use the story trail to encourage your child to retell the story in the right sequence, in their own words.

Support comprehension by asking your child to tell you about the story.

Help your child think about the messages in the book that go beyond the story. Ask: "Can you think of other creatures that might need help finding food in winter?"

Give your child a chance to respond to the story: "Did you have a favourite part? Did you expect the robin to take any of the food? Why/why not?"

Extending learning

Help your child extend the story structure by using the same sentence pattern and adding some more elements: "There might be other food items the boy could offer the little robin. 'I held out a nut. Come here, robin.' Now you think of one."

On a few of the pages, check your child can finger point accurately by asking them to show you how they kept their place in the print by tracking from word to word.

Help your child to use letter information by asking them to find the interest word on each page by using the first letter. For example: "Which word is 'slug'? How do you know it is that word?"

Franklin Watts
First published in Great Britain in 2023 by Hodder and Stoughton
Copyright © Hodder and Stoughton Ltd, 2023

Series Editors: Jackie Hamley and Melanie Palmer
Series Advisors and Development Editors: Dr Sue Bodman and Glen Franklin
Series Designers: Cathryn Gilbert and Peter Scoulding

A CIP catalogue record for this book is
available from the British Library.

ISBN 978 1 4451 7451 8 (hbk)
ISBN 978 1 4451 7452 5 (pbk)
ISBN 978 1 4451 8550 7 (ebook)

Printed in China

Franklin Watts
An imprint of
Hachette Children's Group
Part of Hodder and Stoughton
Carmelite House
50 Victoria Embankment
London EC4Y 0DZ

An Hachette UK Company
www.hachette.co.uk

www.reading-champion.co.uk

FSC
www.fsc.org
MIX
Paper from
responsible sources
FSC® C104740

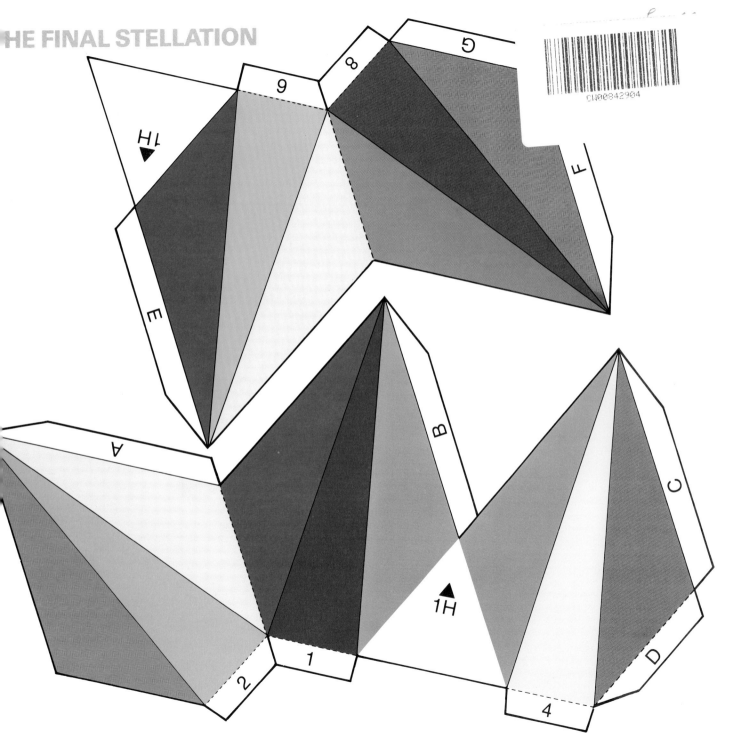

G

F

E

B

C

A

D

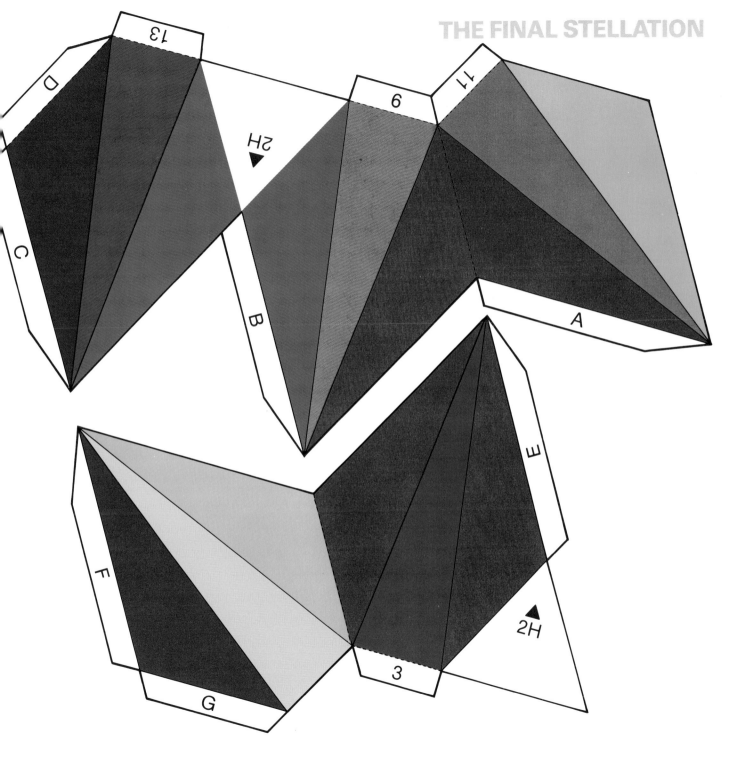

A

B

C

D

E

F

G

1

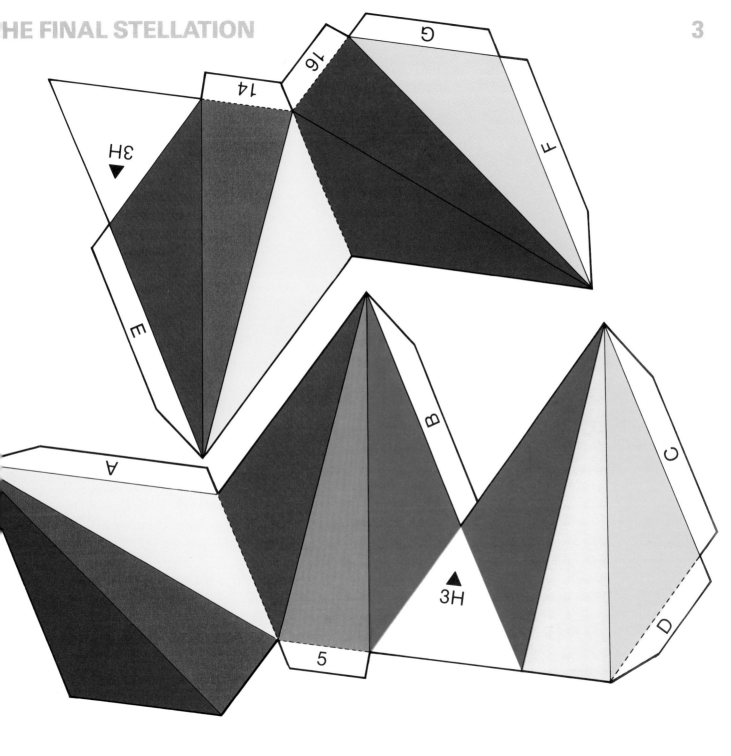

G

F

E

B

C

A

3

2

D

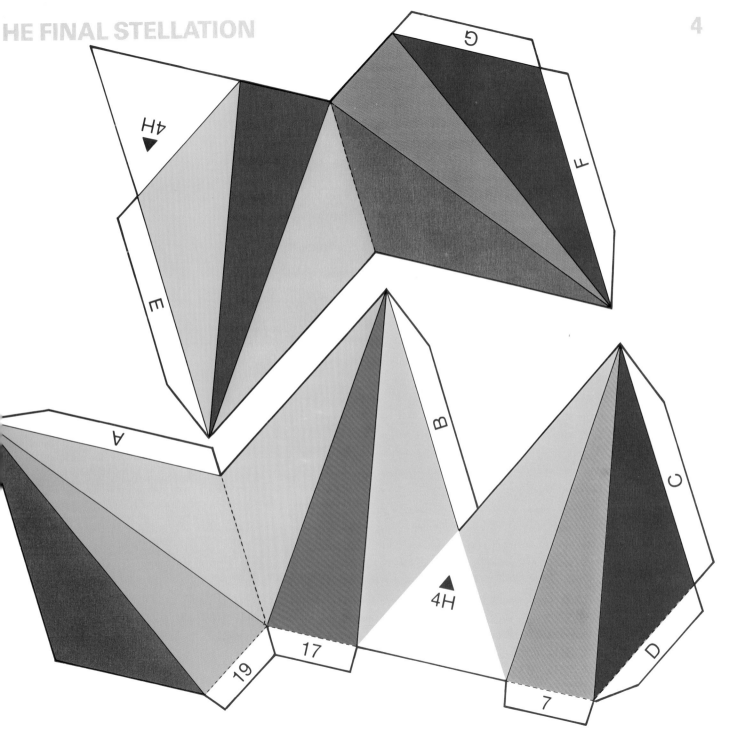

5

4

G

F

E

B

C

A

D

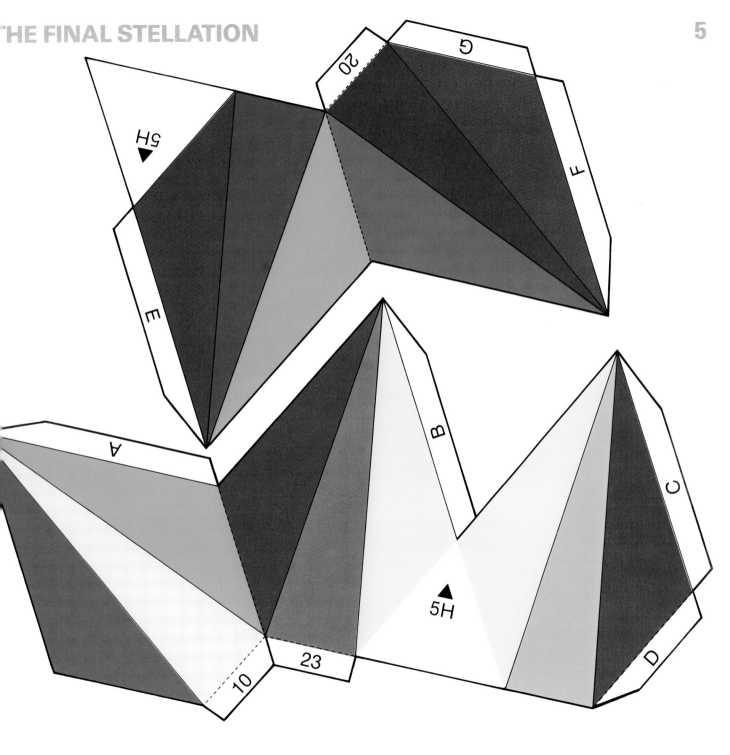

L

G

F

E

B

C

A

6

D

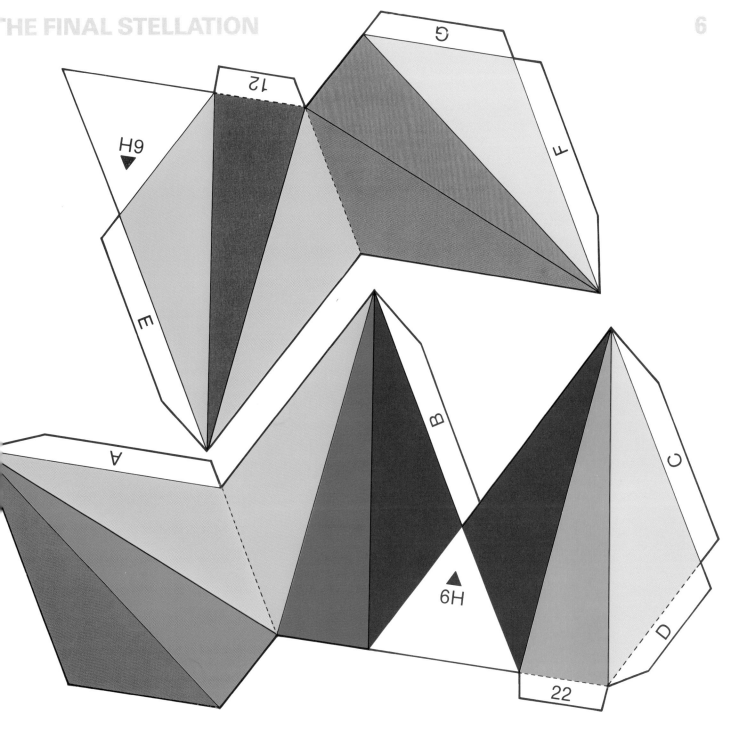

6

G

F

E

B

C

A

8

10

D

E

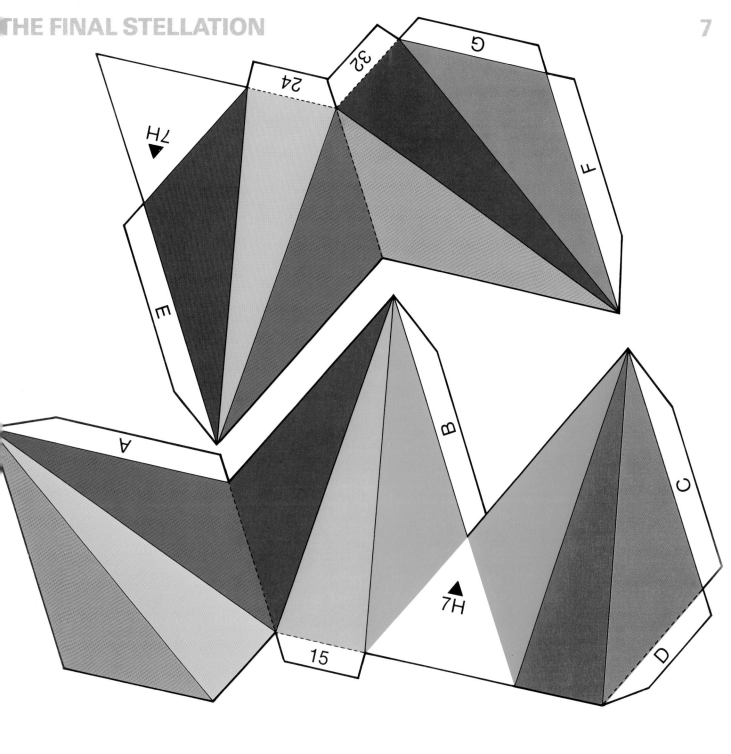

G

F

E

B

C

A

11

D

12

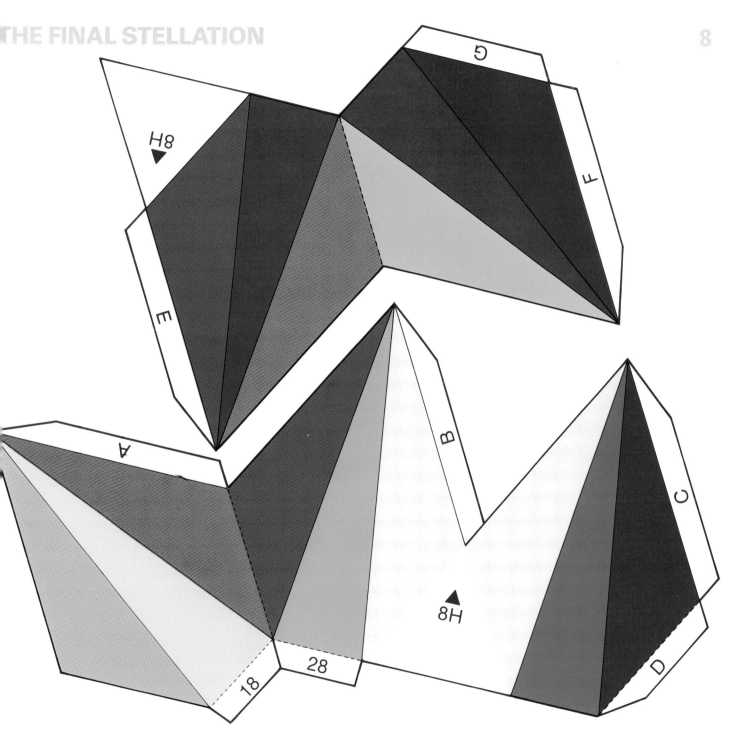

15

13

G

F

E

B

C

A

D

14

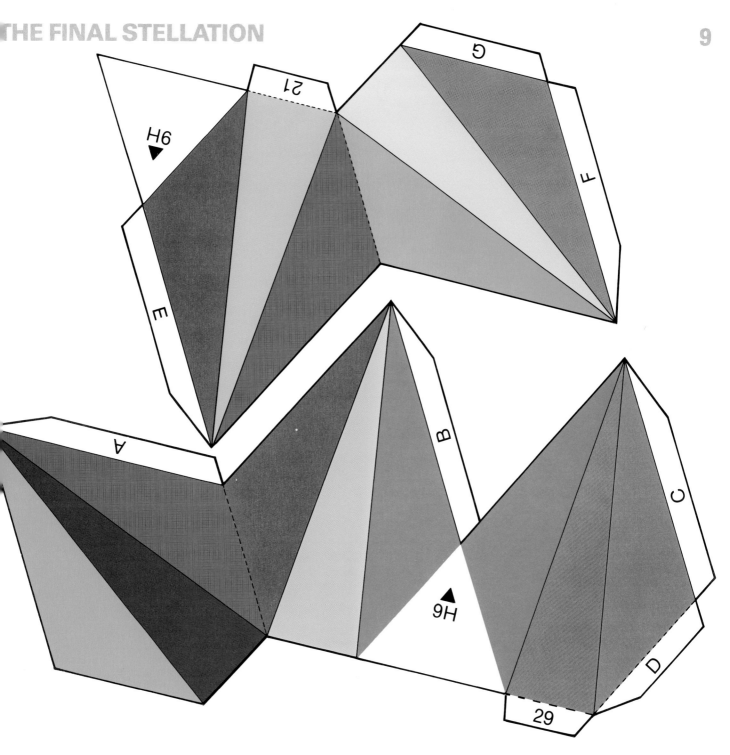

H6 ▲

21

E

G

F

A

B

▲ 9H

C

29

D

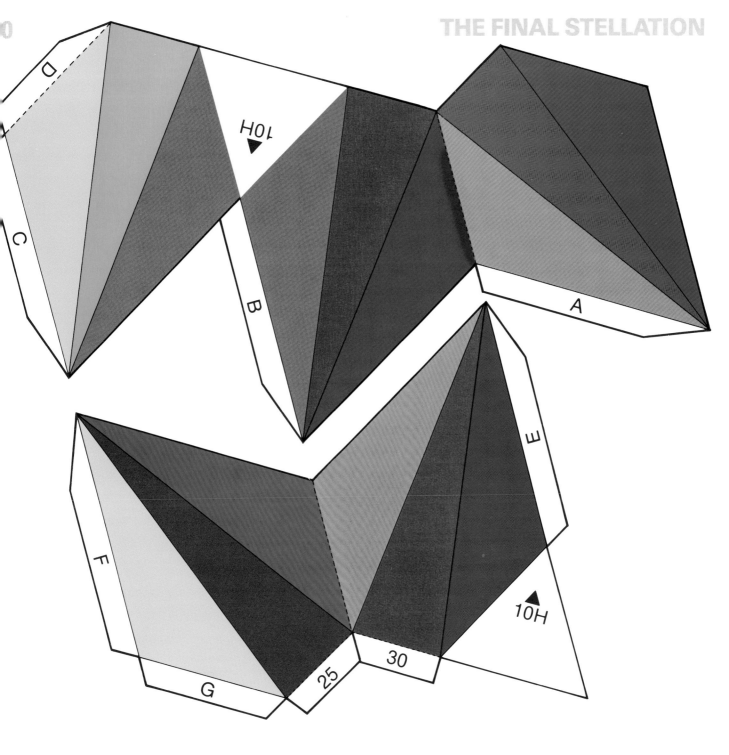

A
B
C
D
E
F
G
19
20
21

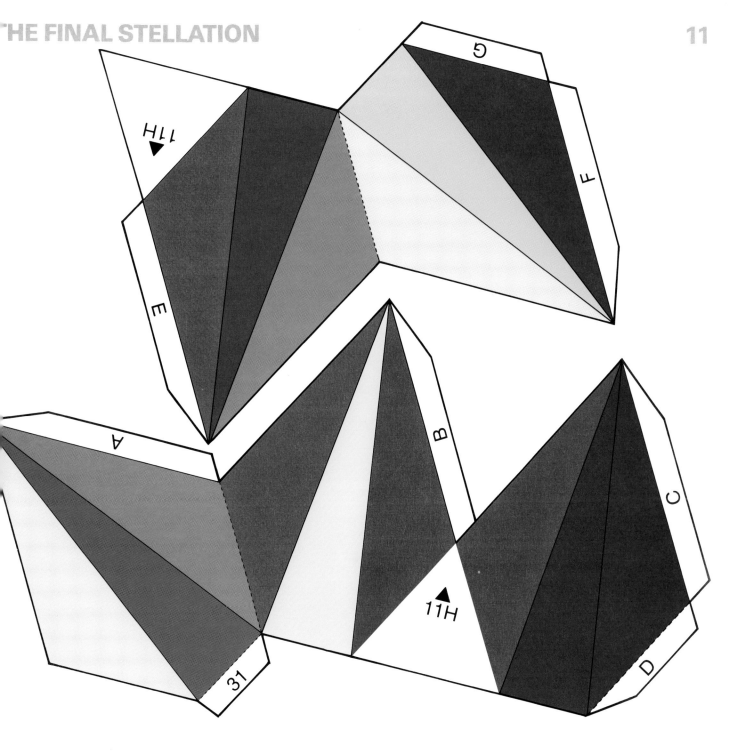

23

22

G

F

E

B

C

A

25

D

24

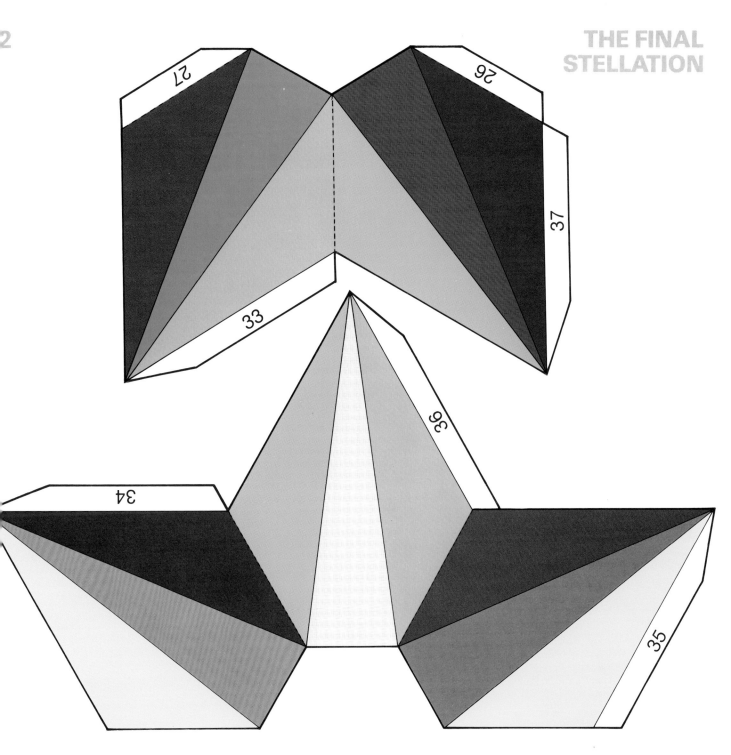

29

30

33

37

36

35

32

34

28

31

26

27

Fireman Sam

AND THE TREETOP ADVENTURE

by Caryn Jenner

Illustrations by The County Studio

HEINEMANN · LONDON

Norman, Sarah and James were playing in Pontypandy Park.

"Let's play a guessing game," said Sarah. "I'll pretend to be an animal and you two guess what it is."

Sarah swung her arm in front of her nose like a trunk and made a loud noise.

"I know!" said Norman. "You're an elephant."
"That's right," said Sarah. "Now it's your turn."

Norman couldn't decide what animal to be.
Then he saw a flash of ginger up in the tree.

It was Rosa the cat, who lived at Bella's café.
Rosa loved to climb trees.

Norman grabbed hold of the lowest branch and began climbing. Higher and higher he went.

"You're a bird," called Sarah.
"No, not a bird," said Norman.
"Don't climb too high, Norman," warned James.

"My animal likes to climb very high in the tree,"
said Norman with a grin. "Miaow."

"You're a cat!" guessed Sarah.
"Right you are!" said Norman. "I'm Rosa the cat."

"Come on down now, Norman," called James.
Norman looked down from the tree.

He had climbed even higher than he'd thought!
"I think I'm stuck!" he said.

"Don't worry, Norman," called Sarah. "I'll phone the fire brigade. Uncle Sam will help you down."

A few minutes later, Fireman Sam and Firefighter
Elvis Cridlington arrived at the park in Jupiter.
Dilys Price and Bella Lasagne arrived, too.

"Norman, my precious, is that you?" Dilys called up
into the tree.

With Elvis holding the ladder steady, Fireman Sam climbed up to get Norman.

Carefully, Fireman Sam helped Norman onto
the ladder.
"It-it's a long way down!" Norman gulped.

Step by step, they made their way down the ladder
to the ground. Rosa scampered down the tree
behind them.

"What a brave boy my Norman is!" said Dilys.
"Aw, Mam," Norman groaned.

"Mamma mia, such adventures make me hungry,"
said Bella. "Who wants lunch at the café?"

At Bella's café, everyone enjoyed a delicious lunch, even Rosa.

The cat leaped onto Norman's lap.
"She wants you to play with her," said Bella.

"I'll play with you, Rosa," Norman chuckled, "as long as we don't climb any trees!"